# O God! Why me?

Author

**Acharya Vijay Ratnasundersuri**

*An imprint of*

**B. Jain Publishers (P) Ltd.**
An ISO 9001 : 2000 Certified Company
USA — EUROPE — INDIA

**O GOD! WHY ME?**

First Edition: 2009
1st Impression: 2009

All rights reserved. No part of this book may be reproduced, stored in a retrieval system or transmitted, in any form or by any means, mechanical, photocopying, recording or otherwise, without any prior written permission of the publisher.

© with the author

*Published by Kuldeep Jain for*

**HEALTH HARMONY**
*An imprint of*
**B. JAIN PUBLISHERS (P) LTD.**
An ISO 9001 : 2000 Certified Company
1921/10, Chuna Mandi, Paharganj, New Delhi 110 055 (INDIA)
*Tel.:* 91-11-2358 0800, 2358 1100, 2358 1300, 2358 3100
*Fax:* 91-11-2358 0471 • *Email:* info@bjain.com
*Website:* **www.bjainbooks.com**

*Printed in India by*
**J.J. Offset Printers**

ISBN: 978-81-319-0835-8

# Publisher's Note

This work records a dialogue between a holy saint and young disciple who realizes that the only thing an uncaring, indifferent and cruel society respects, heeds and mimics without questioning is the possessor of riches or one who wields authority on the strength of his office. If a young man is good and kind, he'll be bossed around by all and sundry. If he is talented, brawny and enduring, he will be ignored and universally ridiculed for not possessing a car or a prestigious white collar job. If he is ever ready to help those in distress, need or in trouble, he will be valued only for what the powerful or weather can snatch from him, and none will dare to question or check his increasing isolation lest the powerful or the wealthy feel offended.

To these questions, Acharya Vijay Ratnasundersuri has customized responses. Gold is tested in the fire, and acceptable men in the furnace of humiliation.

Publisher's Note

Acharya Vijay Ratnasundersuri is one such saint who has torched the life of millions and changed their world altogether. We as a publisher are very happy to publish his works and take this message to a wider readership.

**Kuldeep Jain**
*CEO, B. Jain Publishers (P) Ltd.*

# About the Author

Sarasvati Nandan Param Poojya Acharya Vijay Ratnasundersuri is a renowned Jain Saint. He was born on 5th January, 1948 at Depla (Near Palitana, Gujrat). In spite of being a religious saint, he wrote many visionary books for the socio-cultural upliftment of individual as well as society at whole. Till today, he has written more than 230 books in his mother tongue (Gujarati). Many of these books have

## About the Author

been translated in various languages such as English, Hindi, Urdu, French etc., and more than 33,00,000 circulations of his books are spread over the nation.

He gives Pravachan (lecture on morality and spirituality based Personality Development). Through his writings and speeches, he has achieved success in bringing about positive and constructive changes in millions of people and that is why these millions of Indians follow his ideals.

Being a Jain saint, author follows very hard rules and regulations. He walks barefoot and has not taken bath since 1967 when he adopted saint ship which is called 'Diksha'. He does not eat and drink after sunset till sunrise. Thus, he is not only an author or lecturer but a motivator as well and teaches us that discipline and dedication can make you more empowered.

# Preface

## Madness - Misery - Prudence

The great misunderstanding of our mind is that all comforts are because of our efforts and all discomforts are because of other people. Having this attitude, it gives all credit of comforts to itself and disgrace of discomforts to others. Consequently, it falls a prey to madness when in comfort and becomes a victim of misery when in discomfort. The only solution to this problem is prudence and wisdom. This can be obtained by the grace of God.

With the grace of God and with my little knowledge I have tried here to explain how one can be placid during comforts and happy during discomforts.

I can't make out why highly spiritual persons also become victims of the thought that despite doing so many good and noble deeds, they have to

## Preface

face many problems. I have just tried to eliminate this misconception.

I am fully confident that many would get some solution from this book. Finishing this preface, I beg pardon if I have transgressed any doctrine of Jainism.

Acharya Vijay Ratnasundersuri

# 1

**Sir,**

I am disturbed with a question and I must get the answer. Otherwise whatever is good and noble in my life may vanish. Here is the problem. Is it the rule of the world that, 'One who is good, who retains goodness and who walks over the noble path always has to suffer miseries, difficulties, insults & injustice ?'

You just bow and people will bend you. You preserve morals and people will consider you orthodox. You become honest and you will remain poor. You practise self - restraint and society will consider you backward. You place religion at the foremost and people will place you last. This question may be common to many but I surely have the pain, the agony and the torment. Always a single and same question repeatedly arises in my mind 'Why all difficulties befall only upon me?' 'Why injustice to me only?' 'Why insults to me only?' 'Why all suffering only in my share?' 'Why only I am suppressed?' 'Why only I am to shed tears upon my misfortune?' Please answer my question and remove my predicament and please put an end to my agony.

Naman

# 2

**Dear Naman,**

I read your letter patiently. Before answering your question, I would like to ask you some questions. Just tell me which stone gets more chisel strokes, an idol stone or a mill stone? Who has the misfortune of being trampled under the feet, a thorn or a flower? Who has to pass the test of fire, iron or gold? Who has to suffer more, a wise man or a mad man? Who has to practise more restraint, a prostitute or a chaste woman? Who has to fear from the bandits, a beggar or a wealthy man? I am sure about your answers: If you want to be a gentle man you must tolerate more miseries than a rogue. If you wish to be truthful, you must suffer more difficulties than a rogue or a loafer. If you desire to be pious, you must definitely bear more difficulties than a sinner. The choice is yours! You are free to choose the option, either to live an easy and long life of a thorn or to live a hard but short sweet life of a flower.

Yours

# 3

**Dear Naman,**

According to the law of gravitation, I would like to draw your attention that when one wants to rise above the earth, the force of gravitation pulls him down. Therefore, one who wants to get up from bed would have to bear more strain than one who wants to sleep on the bed. Similarly one has to bear more strain in standing, in walking, in running and in jumping. If a rogue wishes to turn into a gentleman, if one wishes to change his worst nature into a best one, then obviously he has to have more pain, more difficulties, more insults and more injustice. You might have heard the proverb 'One who lights a lamp in a thieves' den becomes an enemy of the thieves'.

This proverb clearly states that thieves have thick friendship with darkness, so how can they tolerate the illuminator? Thus the ignorant class of this world like immorality. How can they tolerate the person advancing towards nobility? How can they greet them?

Yours

# 4

**Sir,**

Reading your two letters, some of my misconceptions were removed. However, my question is that although we walk on the straight path why does anguish come? After stepping on the path of nobility, why do difficulties come? If stating frankly one who walks on the path of immorality lives merrily. On the other hand for one who walks on the path of nobility, only anguish, discomforts and difficulties become part and parcel of his life.

If it is the rule that, 'one who performs noble deeds reaps happiness in life' then why am I unhappy? And if 'one who commits sins gets pain' then why are sinners happy? Do you have any reply to these questions?

Naman

# 5

**Dear Naman,**

Comforts bear a positive relationship with noble activities. But, this doesn't mean that as you do noble deeds so you get its fruits simultaneously. If you sow a mango seed today, it will reap mangoes after some years. Similarly, if you sow the seeds of noble deeds today, you shall reap its fruits after a period of time.

Similarly, misery bears a positive relationship with sin but this doesn't mean that the moment you commit a sin, misery falls upon you. Just as the bitter seeds of a neem tree sown in the soil today bear bitter fruits after an interval of time, a sin committed today shows its results after a period of time. In short, you feel sweetness as soon as you put sugar on your tongue. But as soon as you perform noble deeds, you can't get happiness.

Your hand burns as soon as you put it in fire. But misery does not assault you as soon as you commit sins. May I explain to you in your language? Almond does not transform into blood as soon as it is eaten.

Similarly, you do not face the problem of loose motion immediately after you have over – eaten. Applying this rule over here you do not obtain happiness the moment you perform noble deeds nor does misery fall upon you as soon as you commit a sin. You are an intelligent fellow. In accordance with the solution given above, you find an answer to the question I asked you and also find out an answer to the question that you have asked me. It is possible for a noble person to be distressed, tormented and worried although he performs many noble deeds.

This irony just states that the sins committed by him intentionally or un-intentionally in his previous births are showing their results today. Like wise, although one is leading a sinful life today, he might be happy, comfortable and wealthy.

This contrast reveals that he is probably enjoying the fruits of the religious practices or noble deeds performed by him in his previous births.

Yours

# 6

**Dear Naman,**

A man wants the results of noble deeds immediately but never wants the fruits of even a single sin. Should I tell you the truth? The noble deeds performed by either you or me in our life time would be meagre, 1 or 2% whereas the sins committed by us in its comparison would be around 98%. If noble deeds and sins, both bear fruit immediately, what would be our situation?

Not even an ounce of happiness in our share and to add fuel to the fire the onslaught of tons of misery. You ought to be grateful to the law of nature for maintaining the policy, where-by our actions, whether good or bad don't bear fruits immediately. After understanding this fact, you will surely say, 'Oh God ! I am not complaining to you for not rewarding my good deeds immediately but I am very grateful to you for not punishing me immediately for my sins.

Yours

# 7

**Sir,**

I admit that pleasures are obtained by performing noble deeds and misery is obtained by committing sins but after an interval of time. But confusion still persists in my mind that this will make a person negligent in performing noble deeds.

He might think that even if he performs noble deeds now, he won't get its fruits in the near future, then why should he perform it ? On the other hand he might become shameless in committing sins. He will think that even if he commits any number of sins, he won't get its fruits in the near future. Then, why shouldn't he enjoy now? Do you have any answer to this?

Naman

# 8

**Dear Naman,**

May I ask you a question? Have you opened a F.D (Fixed Deposit) A/c in a bank any time? If so, why? With the expectation that the amount deposited today would double after some years and it would be useful then. Now tell me, if you had opened this F.D. happily or sadly? Did any one force you to open the F.D? Or did you get it done yourself? If you can open an F.D. happily with the expectation that the amount will double after some years then your fear that a person will lose interest in performing noble deeds if he doesn't get immediate results, is not logical.

Tell me, who is not anxious for a safe and better future? The day a person develops deep faith that 'Performance of noble deeds alone has the capacity to make my future safe', he shall not halt even for a moment in performing noble deeds. What more do

I tell you? Man believes that wealth brings security therefore he runs 24 hours after it. Similarly, if he visualises safety in the performance of noble deeds; he will undoubtedly perform noble deeds at any cost, come what may.

Yours

## 9

**Dear Naman,**

Have you seen fancy pouches of mouth-fresheners and tobacco at betel-leaf stalls? Though you know that its ingredients are delicious and fragrant, you never tasted them at all. Why? Because you are aware that tobacco is an invitation to cancer.

Your understanding is crystal clear in this respect. Mouth-fresheners might be delicious momentarily but in the long term it causes cancer. So, you don't even taste it. Same rule applies with regard to commission of sins. The sins committed today might not cause us pain or distress immediately, but in due course it will surely cause suffering and distress. If this belief is deep rooted in your heart, then you will never tread on the wrong path at any cost. What else do I tell you? A person shivers at the very thought of distress. Probably a normal tumour appears in the throat but if the physician tells him in a serious tone to get it checked at the Tata hospital, the patient might start shivering with suspicion that he might be suffering from cancer. He might even lose his sleep due to this suspicion.

If just the imagination of sorrow dejects the person to such a great extent, then wouldn't the deep – rooted belief that 'Commission of sin is an invitation to sorrow' keep him miles away from sin? Investment of money in F.D. and intake of mouth-fresheners give its results in this life itself, as such man instinctively becomes involved in it or disassociated with it. However, a person does not easily give up sins nor undertake good deeds because he does not reap the reward / punishment of noble deeds/sins in this life but in the coming lives. As such man's belief in this regard doesn't stabilize soon. If your belief in the benefit of religion and the harm in committing sin is stronger in comparison with the belief in the benefits of F.D. and the harm of mouth-fresheners intake, then you can't forgo religion and you can't commit sin.

Yours

# 10

**Sir,**

Why the fruits of noble deeds and sins are obtained after a period of time? Isn't it possible to gain an immediate result of both noble deeds and sins? A sweet consumed now transforms into blood after a period of time but its delicious taste can be experienced immediately. Why isn't it so in the case of noble deeds? Repayment of money borrowed on interest is invariably a painful effort after the period of time but the burden of repayment is on the head the moment one borrows money. Doesn't a person experience similar pain while committing a sin?

Naman

# 11

**Naman,**

Your question is good. Assume that you are going from Delhi to Mumbai by train. A week before you had reserved the ticket. Now, give me an answer. It might take you 18-20 hours to reach Mumbai from Delhi by train. Do you have any fear of a Ticket Checker during this period? What does this event indicate? It tells us that on journey the ticket in our purse constantly provides us fearlessness. This is the answer to your question.

The noble deeds grant a good place in the next birth or salvation in the long run, but instantly it grants us fearlessness and happiness. Have you heard this verse ? 'When we worship God, we gain happiness' as you worship God, as you practise his doctrines, so your mind experiences more and more happiness. What else do I tell you? Compared to inner happiness and bliss, all the worldly pleasures seem insignificant and all the worldly distress impotent. Becoming aware of this instant result of doing noble actions, who would postpone performing religious /noble deeds?

Yours

# 12

**Dear Naman,**

Assume that you are travelling without ticket from Delhi to Mumbai, in a train. What will be your mental condition? If any passenger boards the train from any station and gazes at you, you will suspect him to be a Ticket Checker. You will be gripped with fear. In your journey, the weather might be pleasant but the fact that you are 'without ticket' scares you, grips you with fear and as a result your body perspires.

Similarly, the immediate result of committing a sin is FEAR. Though your sin is a preserved secret, though none can know about this, probably you are successful in hiding it deceitfully but still in the court of your conscience you see yourself as a culprit.

The memory of your committed sins will make you a victim of inferiority complex. Inner happiness gives us the strength to bear the onslaughts of misery. Whereas all the pleasures of life seem insignificant if the mind is gripped with fear / phobia.

You just look at this world. Multimillionaires who are dealing with billions are always anxious and scared. They don't have true appetite; they can find 'peace' in a dictionary only. They might enjoy true sleep in a dream only. What is the reason? Their wealth, their status, their prosperity and their fame is tainted with the commission of wrong deeds and sins. Which fear doesn't haunt them?

They are scared of not just their car driver but their official staff too. Probably they are scared of their son too and in solitude they are scared of their conscience. If you are constantly aware of this immediate result of sin, you can't commit sin.

Yours

# 13

**Sir,**

You have given a great solution. A joyous mind is the immediate result of noble deeds and a frightened mind is the immediate result of sins. But may I ask you a question? I'm living happily now. But at times, when sorrow knocks at the door, when distress comes into my life, when I fall a prey to injustice, when I'm forced to face insults for no faults of mine, I become upset and my mind starts moping. Why is it that only I have become the victim of injustice, suffering and pain? Despite tremendous efforts I fail to maintain the equilibrium of mind or the happiness of mind. I would like to have some guidance from you regarding this problem.

Naman

# 14

**Dear Naman,**

Remember, it's not the sorrow that disturbs you but it's the refusal to accept it peacefully that disturbs you. Distress is like a log of wood. It might be heavy and huge. But if you pour water below it or put it in water it becomes light to carry. Likewise, though distress is like the logs of wood, accept it i.e. bring the water of acceptance below it.

Then it can neither trouble you nor disturb you. Never forget that none in this world is completely free from distress, disturbance and discomfort. If a rogue is suffering from distress, then a gentleman too is not free from it.

If men are facing problems women too are caught in the web of problems. The victims of sorrow are not just sinners but gentlemen too. However, those who have accepted these difficulties, discomforts and distress, they are living peacefully and happily amidst all. But, those who have refused to accept distress, are upset and unhappy. Just give me an answer, what is your attitude towards distress? Are you ready to accept it or are you refusing it?

Yours

# 15

**Sir,**

I read your letter three times. It's very easy to write, speak about or inspire others to accept sorrow, but it is very difficult to train the conscience to accept it. Given appropriate and valid reasons the mind gets ready to accept. But, if you are treading on the right path and a rogue harasses you for no obvious reason or if someone puts you under a heavy loss out of jealousy, the mind refuses to accept the pain and stress, paying no heed to your explanations. May I ask you a question? Don't you feel that the tendency of the mind to accept distress might make it feeble? 'Love those who trouble you,' won't this tendency encourage others to do injustice to us?

Naman

## 16

**Dear Naman,**

Look at the lives of the gods, saints and gentlemen. When distress attacked them, they maintained the policy to accept it. When some one troubled them, their attitude was to love them. Do you want to say that by accepting sorrow they became feeble or by loving their enemy they encouraged them to do evil? You will realize that your hesitation to accept sorrow and inclination to punish the wicked has incited you to put forth wrong arguments.

You can't make furniture out of a piece of a wood without cutting it. A person cannot become a gentleman without giving love and accepting sorrow.

Yours

# 17

**Sir**

I admit that the weakness of my mind incited me to argue. However, there must be a limit to the tolerance power of the body and the mind. How much can one tolerate? How long can one tolerate? Whose injustice to tolerate? Must we tolerate the injustice of one and all throughout our lives?

Naman

# 18

**Dear Naman,**

You might not possess pleasure of the prosperity but neither do you have the grievance of poverty. You might not possess sharp eyes but neither are you blind.

You might not be in the pink of your health but neither are you suffering from cancer. You might not be famous in your social circle but you are also not tainted with any stigma. Your family members may not be obedient but neither are they disloyal. Give me an answer. Are you well aware of this reality? What do I write to you? I listened to a song sung by a little blind baby, some time back. Its theme was so much touching that tears started trickling down my eyes while listening to it.

It reads as follows 'O God?' I can feel the sunlight, but I'm not lucky enough to see the sun! I can smell the fragrance of the flower, but I do not have the privilege to look at them! I can hear the thundering sound of the sea but I'm not fortunate to see it ! 'O God!' At last, do I tell you the most tragical story of my life ? I can feel the loving touch of my mother's hands, but I can't see her loving face! Naman, do you have any such grief? Do you have the misfortune to suffer such lamentations? If 'no', then I ask you to go to God and tell him, 'O God ! I don't have any complaint for not getting many pleasures, but I am very thankful to you for not having so many grievances.'

Yours

# 19

**Sir,**

When I read your letter, I realised that my life though lacking in many comforts, is free from many discomforts too. Till now my attention was drawn towards the comforts I lacked, resultantly I was miserable. But today, for the first time my attention turned towards the discomforts which never touched me and I heaved a sigh of relief.

This optimistic outlook has reduced the burden of my mind and relieved me.

Thank God! I didn't become a victim of mental torture. Will you please explain in depth on this topic?

Naman

# 20

**Dear Naman,**

I am not referring to the conduct of your previous life, but I am asking you whether in this life, whether the majority of the deeds performed by you are noble or sinful? Have you utilized your tongue more in eulogy or in abuse? Was your mind pre-occupied most of the time with noble thoughts or vicious thoughts? Were you planning most of the time for good deeds or evil deeds? Probably your answer would be as such, the proportion of immaterial, irrational, inauspicious and immoral acts in life is in abundance and the proportion of appropriate, meaningful, good and pious acts is less. If the balance sheet of the present life is such, then what can one say about the previous births? What does it mean?

The sins you have committed in your life are enormous whereas the noble deeds are much less. If this reality is noticed by you, then you will never complain about misery in your life. On the other hand you will say 'Only this much misery in my share?'

Yours

## 21

**Dear Naman,**

Stop asking 'though I tread on the path of truth why so much distress in my share?' Rather start asking 'though I tread on the wrong path many times, why only this much distress in my share?'

Yours

## 22

**Dear Naman,**

Do you know the weakness of the mind? Though the misery is little, it appears huge. Though the pleasure is in abundance it appears little. Due to this distorted vision man is always dissatisfied, worried and tensed up. However, the reality is that happiness lies in the feeling of gratitude. But, if a person is given to complain all the while how can he experience happiness, peace, serenity and sound health? 'So much misery in my share' is the attitude of complaint. 'Only this much misery in my share' is the attitude of gratitude. I like to tell you that whenever distress, discomforts and difficulties fall on you, apply this principle.

The resultant placidity and serenity you would experience is beyond your imagination. In my discourse, I often quote an anecdote, which I am putting forth before you. A youngster of Delhi went

## O God! why me?

to the market alongwith his friend who came from Mumbai.

A cyclist coming from behind hit him, blood started oozing out from the affected area. But the moment his eyes fell on the cyclist his eyes shone with delight. He went near the cyclist and thanked him a lot. His friend was greatly surprised with his reaction. He asked him, 'Dear friend, do you know that you are thanking the person who hit you and injured you?'

'Yes'

Why?'

I know him well. Generally he drives trucks, I am very fortunate because he was riding a bicycle today.

Yours

# 23

**Sir,**

You have reduced the burden of sorrow by showing the bright horizon of deep insight. Besides the short time of sorrow you have sketched a very long line of deep insight, resultantly the sorrow has become insignificant. Earlier my torment was 'so much sorrow in my share?' But now my amazement is 'only this much sorrow in my share?' What more can I tell you at this moment? But I can assure you that from now onwards in the future if misfortune befalls me, I will neither become desperate nor will I complain. For the first time I have realized the inherent strength of deep insight.

Though, the situation today is the same as before, I feel that I am at the top of the world. I am experiencing the tremendous power of deep insight for the first time in my life. I am very thankful to you for providing me the key to limitless treasures of happiness free of cost! Please, give me your blessings, so that this deep insight may not be just an outburst, but outlast my life.

Naman

## 24

**Dear Naman,**

It is easy to reconcile the mind to accept distress happily in favorable circumstances, but it is difficult to maintain composure in the time of distress. This is a challenge not just for you in your life but for me too. Hence, let's pray to God and request Him not to lighten our burden but to strengthen our will power and inner strength.

Yours

# 25

**Dear Naman,**

I would like to remind you that acceptance of distress alone is not the key to inner happiness but an attitude of gratitude for the comforts received is the infallible key to inner happiness. May I tell you a weakness of the mind? It always thinks 'only this much pleasure in my share?' 'I possess only one car but not three?' 'I have only a flat, but not a bungalow?' 'I own just Rs. 1 Crore, but not Rs. 5 Crore?' 'I am just a trustee of the institute, but not the President?' 'I am popular only in my family, but not in the whole society?' 'The furniture in my flat is worth five lakh rupees but not fifty lakh rupees ?'

The mind is always burdened with the illusion that it possesses very few comforts. Due to this dissatisfaction man is never happy. Probably you might also have become a victim of such distorted thinking; resultantly happiness is miles away from you. In this context I would like to give an excellent solution.

You are dejected because you feel that the happiness in your share is very little. From now on you ask your mind, 'how is it that the happiness in my share is so very much?' 'When I don't know how to make the best use of my eyes, how has fate given me good eyes?' 'When I don't possess the skill to invest my wealth in the lucrative sectors, how have I become a millionaire?' 'When inauspicious thoughts play havoc in my mind most of the time, how can I have a sound mind?' 'Alas! I lack the technique of praising the virtuous, how can I possess an eloquent tongue?' 'I do not possess a warm heart, how can I expect to win the heart of my family and friends?' 'In fact, I am neither virtuous nor am I fortunate, yet God has granted me a lot. On what basis?' In short one can't get a necklace worth one lakh rupees by paying just a hundred rupees, similarly, in this or in past birth I didn't amass any punya (Punya-merit earned by performing noble deeds) yet how has providence provided me so many pleasures? Did you ask yourself these questions any time?

Yours

# 26

**Dear Naman,**

All the pleasures available to me or to you today – sharp eyes and ears, fluency of the tongue, strong and healthy hands and legs, sound mind, money enough to satisfy our necessities, clothes enough to cover our body decently, food enough to satiate our hunger, a comfortable house to live in, it's all due to the generosity of the Karma – Satta (Karma Satta: natural administration of cause and effect reality) but certainly not due to our credit worthiness.

You inscribe this reality on the walls of your heart. If in case, by mistake dissatisfied with your present condition you offer your papers to karma satta for re – checking, it is probable that you might lose even the meagre pleasures you are enjoying now.

Yours

# 27

**Sir,**

An assimilation of your last two letters shocked me. Two blazing questions kept disturbing me many times since many years. One is 'so much distress in my share?' and the other is 'so little pleasure in my share?' You have provided an excellent solution to these two questions, 'only this much distress in my share?' and 'so much pleasure in my share?' Looking at the water flowing out of the tap we can make a fair guess regarding the quality of water in the tank.

Similarly, watching the mode of speech, action and thought process of a person we can make an assumption of his nature in the previous birth. An introspection of my life shows that the sorrow coming in my share is less than the quantum of evil deeds committed by me and the pleasures I enjoy today are greater in comparison with the noble deeds performed by me.

If this is the reality then why should I be dejected, impatient, harassed, offended or unsatisfied even for a moment? In the spur of joy I feel like approaching God at this very moment and thank him for reducing the punishment for my evil deeds and increasing the award of my noble deeds. I am at a loss of words to express my gratitude for the benevolence showed by Him.

The fact is that if I can't maintain my equilibrium now amidst minor discomforts then what would be my position when I receive a full - fledged punishment for my evil deeds? Likewise, amidst so many pleasures if I can't experience happiness then what would be my condition when I'm awarded happiness in accordance with quantum of noble deeds performed by me.

Naman

## 28

**Dear Naman,**

I read your letter. I am very pleased to know that you have established the roots of deep insight firmly in your heart. Maintain this divine insight amidst the onslaught of distress, rampage of difficulties and abundance of luxuries. My hearty blessings are with you. However, I would like to draw your attention towards the fact that whenever you see comforts, pleasures, joy or amusement in the life of others, be rest assured that it is the result of his religious practices in the previous birth. The sign of the holy flag signifies the existence of a sacred temple. Likewise in the backing of each pleasure, there must be some noble deeds.

It is possible that such a person might be committing sins all the time in the present life. He might be indulging in the heinous crime of brutal murder or adultery, he might be a thief and also a hypocrite, a cheat and also a dacoit, a rapist and also a hunter and yet he might be enjoying the greatest of pleasures, he might be the indisputable monarch of the entire world. I am drawing your attention towards this fact especially because people now a days have the misconception that in this age sinners are enjoying and noble men are suffering. You can achieve happiness only by treading on the wrong path and you face just distress walking on the path of truth. I don't want you to become a victim of such an illusion. As sweetness has direct relationship with sugar and bitterness has direct relationship with neem. So, pleasure has direct relationship with noble deeds and distress has direct relationship with sins. How can you close your eyes to this eternal truth?

Yours

# 29

**Sir,**

You have really touched my Achilles heel. Even after receiving many letters of yours offering a vivid description of the law of Nature and Karma, there is a question continuously hammering my mind. It's that 'If pleasure can be obtained only by performing noble deeds, then why are sinners leading a happy and carefree life? If sorrow is the result of only sin and evil, then why are noble men in distress? I've tried to obtain a solution to this question by putting forth various arguments and explanations before my mind, but to no avail. Please dispel my misconception once and for all.

Naman

# 30

**Dear Naman,**

I am telling this not just to you, but to all those who are under the spell of this misconception that 'all the sinners are happy and all noble men are distressed.' Call a meeting of your family members and tell them 'our goal is to obtain happiness. So, let's bid good bye to religion and start treading on the path of sin and evil.' Addressing your kids, tell them they are all free to do what they like. Grant permission to go to club and discotheques. They are free to come back home at their convenient time. 'We will sit together and watch blue films. My business policy is to amass as much money as possible by hook or by crook. Only thorns are strewn on the path of religion. As such we'll quit it. From now on goodbye to temple, austerities, donation, decent behavior, humility and wisdom. Let's arrange a cremation ceremony of love, sympathy, affection, tolerance.'

'In short let's start committing sins in full force and stop performing religious activities. Why ? Since we want to be pleased and we don't want to be in distress at all'. Naman, I am not talking about others but will you put forward a proposal of this type before your family members ?

Yours

# 31

**Dear Naman,**

What do I write to you ? Even a downright gambler takes care to keep his son away from gambling. An adulteress is ever alert to keep her daughter away from adultery. An elderly person abusing his family members all the time, prevents young ones from speaking offensive language. An elder brother watching vulgar scenes on T.V. keeps his younger brother at bay. A father, though a seasoned liar, slaps his son if he happens to speak a lie, once in a while. Why is it so ? If treading on the path of sins and addiction, there is only enjoyment, pleasure and comforts, then why does a sinner or a chronic addict prohibit his family from treading on that path ? Why does he thwart them ? Why does he scold them ? Why does he punish them, if in case they tread on that path ? It's because the person walking on the path of sin is gifted solely with distress, dejection, ruin and loneliness. For this very reason the parents prevent their children from walking on the path of sin.

Naman, May I tell you a fact ? You are of the opinion that your friend is in the pink of health, but the reality is that body has swollen Your misconception is that your friend looks elegant when he wears shoes, but the fact is that the shoes have wounded his feet. You are of the belief that people earning millions illegally are living merrily, but the truth is that they are living in chronic fear, tension, torment, dejection, guilt and phobia. Some are depressed, some are on the verge of committing suicide.

The world of sin appears attractive, tempting but once you enter it, only sorrow, tears, agony, lamentation and grief come in your share.

Yours

# 32

**Sir,**

I can't make out what to write to you. You have raised an issue in the last letter 'If sinners are happy, then why aren't you ready to make your family sinful?' I don't have any answer to this question. Not just I but all those who nurture the belief that sinners are always happy will fail to give an answer to this question.

You have rightly pointed out that no parent will allow his children to tread on the sinful path. Which parent is not worried lest his child be caught in the jaws of bad company? Which parent is not anxious lest his child be mesmerized by the glittering stars of the deceptive world? Which person does not nurture the belief that the legacy of virtues will help the child to withstand the upheavals of life, but not the legacy of wealth? Though this is the fact, yet the mind is attracted by the luxurious lifestyle of sinners. Why is it so?

Naman

## 33

**Dear Naman,**

The mind is always at crossroads with rules, policies and restraint 'You should do this and you shouldn't do this.' 'You can eat these and you can't eat those.' 'You can see these only and you must not see those.' 'You can earn money by fair means, but not by unfair means.' 'You can read this literature and you should not read the other types'.

The mind is least interested in these types of commandments of God and doctrines set up by moral philosophers. Hence, it never hesitates in assuming that sinners living a carefree life are happy. 'May I tell you a bare truth?' This mischievous mind of ours visualises sorrow in the eyes of a chaste woman and happiness in the life of a prostitute.

Yours

## 34

**Sir,**

You are absolutely right. The desire of the mind to be under restriction, control, regulation is next to impossible. Would a monkey desire to sit still in one place for hours together? Would a mad dog like to stay within the boundary of four walls? Would a wild elephant prefer to stay in custody? Would a lustful person desire to maintain a stable and long relationship with any girl? If the answer to all these questions is YES then we can unquestionably say that the mind likes restrictions, controls and limitations.

The questions which remained unsolved for several years, have been solved by your previous letter. Sinner appears happy, gay, and cheerful. But why? It's because he lives an unrestrained life, he doesn't exercise any control over his speech, activities. I feel this must be the reason why the mind believes that noble men are distressed. There are various restrictions upon a noble person.

A noble man lives within the framework of restrictions. He does not eat all that he likes, he doesn't see all that passes before him, he doesn't talk recklessly, he doesn't loiter about aimlessly, he doesn't earn money by illegal means, he is not subjugated by illicit passions. Watching the regulated life of such a person would the mind call him 'Happy?' No, never. It would explicitly call him distressed. Sir! What is your opinion in this regard?

Naman

## 35

**Dear Naman,**

Will a prostitute consider a chaste woman happy? No! Will a base metal consider the gold undergoing smelting process fortunate? Never! Would a dullard consider a rank holder studying day and night lucky? Impossible. Similarly, would a sinner looking at an affluent devotee suffering hardships treading on the path of religion call him 'Lucky or Fortunate'? Impossible. But beware! Just because the inmates of the mental hospital believe that the doctor is not sensible, it isn't necessary for the doctor to part with his sensibility. This concept is easily understandable. Don't you think so?

Yours

# 36

**Dear Naman,**

In context of the sinner and the noble person, I would like to write about an important matter in this letter, so that your misconception in this regard is dispelled totally.

A sinner might have attractive possessions, but alas ! he is never happy nor is he ever satisfied. Devouring the water of tens of thousands of rivers, is the ocean ever satisfied ? Consuming lakhs of tons of wood, is the fire ever content ? Cremating lakhs of corpses, is the cremation ground ever satisfied ?

Similarly, a sinner though amassing millions, flirting around with any number of women, gulping delicious dishes umpteen times, visiting the luxurious hill stations of India and abroad, attaining the highest position of prestige and honour is never satiated, never happy. Ironically, intake of salty sea water aggravates the thirst. Intake of food by a 'Bhasmak' patient acts as an appetizer.

Similarly, the more the amassment and enjoyment of material pleasure, the more the greed for if. Of what use is the intake of water, which increases thirst ? Of what use is the consumption of that food which increases hunger ? Of what use is the possession of those materials which intensify greed ? What is the meaning of enjoying those materials, which increase dissatisfaction ?

Naman, you just test the truth of this statement on the basis of your own life's experience. 'Now stop, it is too much !'. 'Enough, after today not at all !' From now onwards let's put a full stop ! Did you ever raise such a cry of disgust ?

Yours

# 37

**Sir,**

You are absolutely right. Each wholemeal bread consumed satiates the hunger but every material acquired aggravates the hunger of the mind, rather than satisfying it. My experience of the past several years says that in my life permanent satisfaction and steady happiness, these two have become the words to be found only in a dictionary. Inspite of my painful experience of several years what factor is motivating me to run in search of happiness from material possessions?

Naman

# 38

**Dear Naman,**

I am citing an example to answer your question. A young chap named Ramesh, aged 24 years sent his friend Nitin his wedding card. In response, along with the best wishes, Nitin gave him a gift worth Rs.1000. Within six months after receiving the first one, Nitin was surprised on receiving a second wedding card from Ramesh. He called up Ramesh and asked 'what is this'? Ramesh replied, 'Nothing', I just failed in making a proper choice. I like various dishes whereas she likes roaming. How could we adjust ? I divorced her.

Nitin gave him a gift worth Rs. 500 along with best wishes. For the same reason that marriage also failed and Nitin received an invitation card of Ramesh's third marriage. Now, he was furious. He roared 'what is this drama ? Don't you have any shame ?' Ramesh replied with a laugh, 'I was mesmerized by her beauty, but I didn't know that her nature would be so bad.'

She told me 'I won't cook food, I will go to the hotel everyday.' I patiently explained to her in a sweet and calm tone, 'Look, why did I marry you? To add colour to life and to enjoy eating home made dishes. It's not right on your part to refuse to perform your duty.' She walked out on such an insignificant issue and went to her parents home.

**Naman, slavery to passion makes a man nothing but a slave of the person who satiates the hunger of passion.**

Yours

## 39

**Dear Naman,**

After talking with Nitin, Ramesh added 'I might have failed in the selection of my life partner twice, but the girl I chose this time is excellent. If you like to see my choice, you must attend our marriage ceremony.' Nitin cut the line and sent him Rs.100/ as a gift through a messenger. But, just after four months Nitin received his marriage card for the fourth time.

He was vexed. He opened his drawer, picked up a paper and a pen, wrote a sentence in that, folded it and packed it in a cover. He asked his son to give the cover to Ramesh, along with the message to open it in solitude. Ramesh accepted that cover with surprise. He went inside a room and opened it. In it was written **'Victory of hope over experience.'**

Naman, your question was, despite the bitter experiences faced by me many a time in the expectation of satisfaction by material possessions which parameter is enticing me to run in that direction only ? The one and only answer is 'HOPE'. Even after the bitter experience of three marriages, Ramesh took the initiative to marry a fourth lady !

Why ?

Only because of hope. Man nurtures a similar hope in the field of materials. Though, the bitter experience of infinite births displays the stark reality, that the race after materials has gifted him only ash in his hand, man hopes that definitely some miracle might happen in the future and he can attain satisfaction and happiness from materials.

Yours

# 40

**Sir,**

I feel that Ramesh were you, referring to is none else but myself. Ramesh can be called wise, because he has faced the bitter experience with only three women, whereas my foolishness and madness is indescribable because despite the bitter experience of infinite events for infinite time in infinite births, I am also running in search of happiness from material possessions. My race is backed up by the solitary factor 'HOPE'.

Naman

# 41

**Dear Naman,**

Identity loss is inevitable, though the river is aware of the fact, it loves to merge in the sea. Death is inevitable, though the addict knows it, he doesn't stop the intake of the item he is addicted to. Similarly sorrow is inevitable, though the sinner is aware of it he loves to commit sin.

In the previous letter you asked, 'why is our mind inclined to believe that sinners are happy?' It's because the first thought of sin is sweet, immediate effect of sin is sweet and sin is attractive at first look. A dog unaware of the poison mixed in the sweet, eats it happily. Watching his smiling face the other dogs standing near by envy his good luck. Similarly, one who is ignorant of the fact that 'commission of sin is an invitation to intense sorrow', commits sin delightfully.

The ignorant mass watching his delight envy his good fortune. What do I tell you ? One who succumbs to temptation and escapes exertion doesn't just pause with believing that sinners are happy, unfortunately he also believes that noble men are distressed. Why ? He holds the deep rooted belief that one has to face inconvenience while treading on the path of religion and where there is inconvenience, there is nothing else but sorrow. That mind is wretched, which feels that the adulterer is happy and the virtuous is miserable, which believes that a sinner is enjoying and a noble person is suffering.

Yours

## 42

**Sir,**

As far as my opinion is considered, I don't feel that a noble person is distressed, but then, nor do I feel that he is happy. A noble person treading on the path of religion, living with discomforts, suffering distress, facing difficulties and bearing the pain of hunger and thirst, can he be called happy? My mind is unable to accept this fact at any cost. Will you give me guidance in this regard?

Naman

## 43

**Dear Naman,**

It is not the fault of your mind. It is the fault of the misconception, which is deeply settled in your mind. You are of the opinion that all those activities and procedures which enforce restrictions on the mind and prove strenuous to the physical body are painful but not joyful. However in this context I would like to say to you that, 'Please do not commit the fault of fixing the label of "JOY" to all comforts, similarly do not make the mistake of fixing the label of "SORROW" to all discomforts.'

The pleasure of the student watching cricket, despite the approaching examinations is not a 'Pleasure' in the true sense, the agony of a patient staying hungry to regain sound health is not a punishment in the real sense.

The happiness of the dog attained by inserting a bone in the mouth and chewing it is not a 'JOY' in reality, the cries of the patient suffering from post operation pain is not a 'SORROW' in fact. The message is crystal clear. It's not appropriate to impetuously call a sinner happy by just seeing the luxuries of his life, similarly, it's not right to commit the folly of believing that noble people are distressed just by watching the inconveniences or distress faced by them. Don't forget that wherever you go, either in the spiritual field or in the materialistic world, whatever you want, either the possession of materials or to win the heart of a person, you can get the desired result only if you put in efforts. An earthen pot must be ready to bear the heat of the fire, to become strong. A player must be ready to put in tremendous efforts, to become an outstanding player. A forest must be prepared to tolerate the pain of being trimmed at the hands of the gardener, to convert into a beautiful garden. Similarly, a person must be ready to face and welcome distress treading on the spiritual path, to attain salvation.

Yours

## 44

**Sir,**

Reading your previous letter I came to know that, the present day pleasure of the sinner will invariably grant him sorrow in the future.

The present pain and suffering of the noble person will invariably provide him happiness in the future. Am I right ? Please help me to establish this belief firmly in my mind that the pleasures enjoyed by either a sinner or a noble person today is the result of the religious practices of the previous births.

Similarly, the suffering faced by either a sinner or a noble person today is the result of evil deeds performed in the previous births.

Naman

## 45

**Dear Naman,**

Assume that you are going to office from your home. Suddenly, sweet music rings in your ears. You look in its direction and you observe a marvellous scene. You see a huge crowd garlanding a 25 year-old youth. 5 to 7 photographers are continually clicking photographs. Amongst the crowd, some are praising him and some old women are blessing him. What will you imagine while looking at this scene? Of course, you might imagine that this young man must have done some great work due to which he is being felicitated.

Naman, whenever you see a happy person be rest assured that in the past birth, he must have performed noble deeds. If that youth had murdered someone he wouldn't have attained this esteem.

Similarly, if a person had committed only sin in

his past births, there is no possibility of getting pleasures in this birth. However, I would like to tell you that, though the pleasures of today convey the fact that it is a result of noble deeds performed in the past, be cautious, let not the pleasures of today reserve sorrow for the future.

Yours

# 46

**Sir,**

I read your letter three to four times. I was stunned on reading the episode of the youth. It's true that I haven't seen nor have I heard from any one regarding the noble deed performed by him. But the felicitation offered to him indicates that he must have done some noble deed in the past.

You have logically stated that if you see pleasure in the life of anyone today, be rest assured that it is the result of noble deeds performed in the past. Analysing your statement I've come to the conclusion that if luxurious greenery implies the timely watering of plants, if overwhelming fragrance spread in the air expresses the presence of unseen flowers, if the waving of a flag in the air announces the existence of a temple, if the robust health of a person states the consumption of nutritious food, then similarly, the presence of pleasure in the life of a person implies the performance of unseen noble deeds in the past. Am I right ?

Naman

# 47

**Dear Naman,**

I was surprised and elated to know that you could think so deeply and explicitly. You are correct in your thinking. Can you locate any person in this world who doesn't like happiness ? How many persons are aware of the fact that happiness is an inevitable result of noble deeds.

Once each and every living being running in search of happiness realizes that happiness can be obtained only by performing noble deeds, would he wander about in the world shedding religion to obtain happiness ? No, never. Ironically, to obtain pleasures, most of the ignorant people in this world are running for wealth, racing for power, longing to increase material possessions, taking the recourse to wife and family, but they never think of accepting the shelter of religion.

The reason is obvious. They have neither understood nor do they have faith in the statement 'the solitary means of obtaining pleasure is by performing noble deeds' i.e. only religion can bring in happiness. Visualising water where there is not even a drop of water, proves fatal to the deer. Visualising happiness where there is not even an ounce of happiness, paves the way for a miserable future.

Beware !

Yours

# 48

**Sir,**

May I ask you a question? A man is unaware of the fact that pleasures can be obtained by performing noble deeds. But he knows that religion provides solace to the sorrowful. As such, in sorrow, man instinctively takes the recourse to religion.

In happiness, the person is refusing to accept the existence of God, in distress, a man is too busy to visit the saints. In happiness, he refuses to the company of saints. In prosperity the person enjoys in hotels and clubs day and night, while in sorrow, he spends most of his time in religious places to overcome sorrow.

If a man doesn't believe that 'happiness is obtained only by religion' then how does he know that only religion is the saviour of a distressed person ?

Naman

## 49

**Dear Naman,**

This is the strange tendency of the human mind. It doesn't believe that all the pleasures it is enjoying is the result of religion but it believes that its sorrow can be eliminated by religion only. This irony is surprising.

The tendency of the mind to perform noble deeds only in distress is not at all dignified, because it indicates that it is not a lover of religion but is an enemy of distress. When the building is ablaze its owner entreats even his enemy to help him to put out the fire.

Similarly, an atheist takes the refuge of religion to wipe out his sorrows. What does it mean ? If a rogue starts behaving decently with others, agrees to chant God's name, accepts the shelter of saints to overcome his sorrow, it clearly indicates that he wants to escape sorrow by hook or by crook.

O God! why me?

The tendency to resort to religion only in sorrow is not dignified whereas the inclination for performing religious practices even in happiness is graceful. Check your mind. Does it chant God's name only in the temple or in leisure time too ?

Yours

## 50

**Dear Naman,**

May I ask you a question? If a man succeeds in overcoming distress with the help of religion on which path should he tread in happiness? Religious or the sinful one? Why does a man try to overcome sorrow and obtain happiness?

Due to 2 reasons:

(i) Either it is because in distress he can not perform noble deeds or

(ii) Because in distress he can not perform sins.

Assume, that you have 104° degree fever. You can neither go to the market nor to the temple. By taking medicines you want to get rid of the fever at the earliest possible. Why? Is it because you can go to the market or to the temple on becoming healthy? What is your intention? Your answer might be as such. 'I want to obtain happiness and overcome sorrow not because I want to perform noble deeds, but to commit sins.' If our mental attitude is such, it is crystal clear that our mind which takes the refuge of religion in sorrow gives up religion the moment it comes out of sorrow. May I cite you an example? A person was sentenced to five years imprisonment, because he committed a crime. But for some unknown reason everyday in the morning time he used to sing religious songs. Listening to his prayers in his earnest voice, the jailor thought, 'probably this man has accidentally come to jail, but looking at his behaviour it seems that he must have been compelled to commit the crime, in fact he must be a gentleman.' The jailor showing an account of the criminal's good behaviour, requested his chief officer to reduce his punishment.

The next day he received a reply from his chief officer terminating the criminal's punishment and granting him release from jail. The jailor went to that criminal with joy and gave him the good news, 'tomorrow at 8 a.m. you will be freed from the jail' Hearing this news the criminal was elated. But the next day early in the morning when the jailor went to his barrack, he was greatly surprised, because there was dead silence in the room. He couldn't hear the morning prayers. The criminal was in sound sleep. He woke him up, watching the jailor, the criminal stood up immediately. the jailor asked him 'have you been sleeping uptil now ?'

'Yes'

'What about your morning prayers ?'

'No, I don't want to pray ?'

'Why' ?

'The purpose for which I used to sing has been served. Why should I sing now ?' 'What do you mean?'

'I used to sing the prayers to gain an early release from the jail. Yesterday you gave me the good news that I will be released from jail the next day. Oh ! after a long time I slept soundly. Of course, I will sing prayers, but only if I am forced to come here again.' Listening to his reply, the jailor was stunned.

The attitude of a person to do religion only in sorrow motivates him to act in such a manner. As soon as the disease (us) is cured, a patient bids good bye to doctor, medicines, food restrictions. Similarly, an individual performing religion only in distress bids good bye to God, saint, religious practices and religious institutions as soon as he is relieved from distress. How can you call such a person an ardent lover of religion ? However, the person who starts performing religious activities in sorrow, after realizing the inherent strength of religion in wiping out sorrow, might continue performing religious activities even in happiness. But a person who is a victim of the belief 'perform religion only in sorrow' can practise religion but he can't develop an intense liking for religion. What do I say to you ? A drop of oil lying for years together in a vessel filled with water, doesn't mix with water. Where as a drop of water falling in a vessel filled with milk, immediately mixes with milk.

A person who holds the belief 'do religion only in sorrow' might perform religious activities for years together, does not obtain oneness with religion, just like the oil which doesn't mix with water. Whereas the person who holds the belief 'even in happiness do only religion' might have entered the religious world today only, but within no time he obtains one ness with religion just like milk mixes with water immediately. Naman, ask your mind –what does it like ? The oil water relationship or the milk-water relationship ?

Yours

# 51

**Sir,**

After reading your letter, I have concluded that a person who holds the conviction 'do religion only in sorrow' may perform noble deeds in happiness. Whereas a person who is of the conviction 'do religion even in happiness' will invariably perform religious activities either in sorrow or in happiness. I wish to steadily hold the deep rooted belief 'stick to religion even in happiness.'

In the previous letter you logically explained 'at the backing of every pleasure there is only religion' I humbly request you to explain logically. 'The root cause of all sorrow is sin.'

Naman

## 52

**Dear Naman,**

Assume that you are passing by on the road, suddenly you hear someone's scream. Looking in that direction, you see a tragic incident. Some gentlemen are beating a youth aged 25 years severely. 'Rogue ! Aren't you ashamed ?' 'Shameless ! you deserve punishment in jail'. 'You have disgraced your father's reputation.' Speaking like this, they were all beating him. I ask you, what will you infer after seeing all this ? Looking at this, what opinion will you form regarding the youth ? You will definitely infer that 'this youth must have committed an evil deed, hence, this crowd is beating him.' You haven't seen the immoral deed done by him, but looking at the violent response of the crowd, you can definitely infer that he must have committed an immoral deed otherwise such a brutal behaviour is impossible.

Whenever you see sorrow in anyone's life, apply the same logic. A person might not have committed any evil deed, may be viceless, probably he is calm, serene, but, still he might be facing distress, inconvenience, injustice, insults & difficulties. Why is it so ? It's because he must have committed evil deeds in the past.

If smoke can't be seen without fire, if stinking smell can't be felt without the presence of a gutter, then similarly distress can't knock at your door unless you commit a sin. I am sure now you will start believing that, 'where there is distress, there is sin in its backing.'

Yours

## 53

**Sir,**

If there is a flower behind fragrance, there is religion behind pleasures. Along with this faith, I now have strong conviction that there is crime behind punishment and there is distress behind sins. What do I tell you? You have dispelled my illusion. The relief experienced by me today is many times more than the relief felt by a patient on being cured of a disease. I am not overwhelmed with the pleasures available to me, nor am I depressed with the sorrow, inconveniences faced by me.

One question keeps troubling me. What should I do in the present so that in the future sorrow does not knock at my door and happiness does not depart from me? Can you guide me in this regard?

Naman

## 54

**Dear Naman,**

Other things I will tell you later on, but preferably I would like to state you one thing. In this world, each flower of pleasure is surrounded by hundreds of thorns. In this world, happiness is a subject of dreams, whereas sorrow is available in plenty. In this world, superbly laid out plans fail and the unexpected happens.

The book of this world is filled with pages of sorrow wherein appears the thin margin of happiness. If this world is a movie of sorrow, happiness appears in the form of an interval for a short period. What does it mean? An ocean of sorrow and a drop of happiness can be found in this world. If you bear enmity with sorrow and spend all your time in wiping it, when will you do religion ? It's true that, distress is a result of sins committed in the past but it doesn't mean that we fight with it continuously all our life. Trying to eliminate the sorrow of the present you might tread on the sinful path, whereby you reserve distress for the future. His future is miserable, who takes loan to pay interest of previous loan. Likewise, his future is also miserable, who employs sinful ways to eliminate distress. Beware!!

> Yours

## 55

**Sir,**

The mind has a peculiar nature; It creates enmity with what it does not like. You say that we should not create enmity with distress. But the fact is that distress is unwelcome. If we do not adopt a hostile attitude, what kind of an attitude should we adopt towards it?

Naman

# 56

**Dear Naman,**

Do you know? Fire doesn't just burn, it purifies too. Mind doesn't just lead to ruin, it's a saviour too. Poison doesn't just take life, it saves life too. Similarly, sorrow is not just painful, it's beneficial too, it doesn't bring in just suffering, it brings welfare too. Remember this fact every minute of your life. Have you read this verse? 'Distress is the best wealth of a soul'. Distress can prove to be the best wealth, if man knows how to deal with it. What do I tell you? What can you do with the help of wealth? At the most you can buy the most attractive worldly items. But, with the help of distress one can attain supreme knowledge; one can become god, saint or a gentleman. Provide me an answer. Did any one succeed in exposing virtues without greeting or accepting distress, difficulties, discomforts, problems and troubles? No, without facing distress, man can become wealthy, learned, physically strong, a painter and an artist too. But, without facing distress it is not possible for him to become a gentleman, a saint or a god. If the seed of sorrow possesses the potential to yield the fruit of omniscience, then, why do you want to bear hostility with sorrow and lose your life? Wealth provides all sorts of materials and things you want, so you love wealth. Similarly, sorrow exposes the virtues latent in the soul why can't you love it?

Yours

# 57

**Sir,**

The seed of sorrow possesses the potential to yield the fruit of omniscience. Though what you say is true, I am unable to digest your advice and love sorrow. If I dislike thorns how can I love them? I hate disease, then, how can I develop affinity with it? If I am averse to poverty, how can I develop friendship with it? Likewise at any spot or in any circumstance I dislike distress then how could I love it?

Naman

## 58

**Dear Naman,**

Do you like the pain of an operation? No, but still, following the advice of the doctor, you become ready to get operated upon. But why? It's because by bearing the pain of operation once, you expect to get rid of the pain of the disease once and for all. To relieve the body from the pain of disease, the mind agrees to bear the pain of an operation.

Similarly, then to relieve the soul permanently from the pain of distress, vicious mind and birth in hell etc., can't the mind adopt a friendly attitude towards distress coming in the path of religion and adverse deeds ? Since ages, man has felt the pain of only adversities. But from now on you should be vexed with vices & vicious mind. You should experience the weariness of wandering in the world since infinite births.

You should feel the load of deeds and instinctive wickedness. I am sure, the torture, pain and weariness will lead you towards the religious path. It will provide you the power to face the adverse deed; it will motivate you to develop friendship with sorrow. A thorn inevitably pulls out a thorn & an iron inevitably cuts iron. Similarly, friendship with distress will inevitably eliminate distress.

Yours

## 59

**Sir,**

You have given an excellent solution. Till today, it was my belief that just as darkness vanishes in the presence of light, distress disappears by bringing in pleasures only. But you have demolished my belief. To experience pleasure, we should not develop enmity with distress, but we should create friendship with it.

The moment you start loving sorrow, it walks out of your life. This realisation has motivated me to welcome sorrow. But I am in dilemma. When, in reality, sorrow knocks at my door, would I be able to maintain my serenity?

Naman

# 60

**Dear Naman,**

Your confusion is right, but may I tell you one thing? Distress is not as very painful as its rejection. What does it mean? Mind is unprepared to accept sorrow; as such the pain of sorrow is magnified. On the other hand, if the mind is prepared to accept sorrow the pain of sorrow is reduced. If you feel that I am exaggerating, look at me. You are well aware of the fact that our saintly life is full of discomforts. All our life we walk bare footed, maintain celibacy, dedicate our life to our Guru, bear the onslaughts of heat and chill, accept alms only on the fulfillment of many conditions. We pluck our hair with our own hands. Withstanding all these discomforts, I am living a saintly life since 40 years. And yet, these discomforts have never ruffled my mind. Why? The reason is, these discomforts are always acceptable to my mind. I give you the same advice.

You develop friendship with difficulties, discomforts, distress, problems and troubles. Then, look, what great miracles will happen in your life.

Yours

# 61

**Dear Naman,**

May I draw your attention towards a different matter? In our canon texts, there are 3 beautiful verses known to one and all.

1. मित्ती मे सव्व भूएसु – I have friendship with all living beings.

2. खामेमि सव्व जीवे – I forgive all beings of the world.

3. शिवमस्तु सर्व जगत: – I pray for the welfare of all the beings of the world.

When can these three verses be applied practically? If you bear enmity with distress do you think you can make friendship with people who trouble you? Can you forgive people who trouble you? And can you think of the welfare of people who trouble you? Not at all.

The enmity with distress will surely make you an enemy of those people, who were the cause for your distress. The enmity with distresses will create aversion towards those people who have put you in trouble.

This hatred will deprive you from wishing the welfare of those, who were the cause of your distress. The theme of this fact is obvious. If you want to instill the feeling of friendship, forgiveness and desire for the welfare of all beings, then, there is only one highway, develop friendship with distresses.

This friendship with distress will neither make you a victim of ill-will, nor will it make you victim of vicious cycle of thoughts. If the universal truth of mathematics is that $2 + 2 = 4$ only. The universal truth of society is that you can become popular only by performing your duties well. If the universal truth for physical fitness is 'Hunger is the best vitamin' then the universal truth of the spiritual world is that you can become serene, placid, virtuous and good natured only by accepting distress. Now, you must be realizing that as there is no chance of escaping distress in this materialistic world, the only option left is to face it. Similarly, there is no other option left, but, to develop friendship with distress in the spiritual world.

Naman, daringly tell distress, 'you are most welcome!'

Yours

## 62

**Sir,**

Your previous letter dispelled all doubts! I entertained adopting a friendly attitude with sorrow. This world is never void of either sorrow or vicious people. Though, I try my best to avoid, sorrow will collide with me and vicious people will brush with me. Opposing these, I might end up my life, but never succeed. As such, from today, I will not create a wall in front of sorrow, but I will build a bridge. i.e. I will not refuse but accept it. I will not collide with sorrow but I will try to overcome it.

Despite this firm decision of mine, I want to ask you a question. Under any circumstance if it is possible to remove distress, should we welcome distress even then ? Should we develop friendship with it ?

Naman

# 63

**Dear Naman,**

I am not prohibiting you from putting in efforts to remove distress. But as far as I can remember, in a previous letter, I wrote to you that the future of that person, who has to take loan to pay the interest of a loan is bleak. Likewise, the future of that person is dreary, who treads on the path of sin to remove distress. I understand that you are making attempts to wipe out distress coming in your life. But be careful lest it might prove harmful to you. What would be the position of the rat which goes near the cat to escape the agony of a mosquito bite ? The person who treads on the path of sin to get rid of sorrow faces a much more tragic situation than the rat.

Naman, haven't you seen a mango ? After eating it, the left over mango seed can reproduce a new mango. But, what about a banana ? After eating it, no other banana can be reproduced. Enjoy the pleasures in such a manner that it reproduces new pleasure just like the mango fruit. Bear the distress in such a manner, that there is no possibility of reproduction of new distresses, just like the banana.

Yours

# 64

**Dear Naman,**

When we are discussing about the options to be chosen to eliminate distress, let me draw your attention towards an important reality. Assume that electricity goes off suddenly at night in the apartment in which you are staying. You want light in your home at any cost. You try your best to restore it, adopt various means and ultimately you achieve success in your efforts. Let's discuss about another situation. You want to obtain the warmth of sun rays in your apartment after 7 P.M. Whereas the sunset time is 6:45 P.M. You might try your best, but will you succeed in your efforts?

If you challenge a 'sudden event', you may achieve success, but you must accept the 'inevitable'. You can challenge sickness, but you have to accept death. To be relieved from distress you can put in efforts but despite your efforts, if the distress remains as it is, what will you do? You have to consider it as inevitable and accept it. I am explaining this to you because we are living in the world and we are all dependant on our deeds. We can't predict which inauspicious deed bound in which birth might yield its results today.

It is possible that despite your best efforts you can't subside deed and you can't change the situation. If you don't have the deep insight to challenge the sudden and accept the inevitable, then what would be your position? Your mind will become a victim of vicious cycle of thoughts. To relieve your anguish in such a critical situation, I have presented this reality before you.

A farmer can plough his farm, but he can't bring in rains. A businessman can put in efforts to secure an order but he can't be sure of getting it. A man can sleep at night but to wake up is not in his hand. Similarly, you can put in efforts to be relieved from distress but to get success invariably, is not in your hands. Beware!

Yours

## 65

**Sir,**

Reading the two golden lines in your previous two letters, a surge of joy appeared in the heart. The first is, 'do not tread on the path of sin to eliminate distress' and the second is, 'treading on the path of truth, if distress is not eliminated, don't be upset.' To motivate a blind person to get his eye operated to gain sight, is a greater help to him than to motivate him to hold a stick in his hand.

Likewise, providing the right vision through the medium of discourse is a greater obligation than providing suitable material to the distressed and tortured people. What do I tell you? The sorrow, inconvenience & difficulties I am facing today is the same as it was when I started corresponding with you. Yet, I am clearly experiencing positive changes in my mental condition as it was then and as it is now.

The complete credit for this improved mental condition goes to the deep insight instilled by you. I am at a loss for words to express my gratitude for having provided the deep insight.

Naman

## 66

**Sir,**

I promise to tune my life in accordance with advice provided by you in the previous letters which is:-

'Enjoy pleasures in such a way that it can reproduce new pleasures, and bear distress in such a manner that, new distress is not reproduced.'

However, one question which repeatedly troubles me is, 'Will I be able to maintain this deep insight in the time of crisis?' 'Will I be able to face the crisis courageously?' This doubt arose in my mind because I read somewhere that 'in crisis it is very difficult to adhere to the decisions taken in the time of peace.' It's for this very reason I'm scared that 'Will I be able to resist the temptation and stay away from the sinful path when abundant luxuries and unparalleled happiness enriches my life?' 'When unprecedented sorrow knocks at my door, will I commit the crime of shedding the path of Truth?' What is your opinion in this regard?

Naman

# 67

**Dear Naman,**

If you fill water from the sacred Ganges in a tank situated at the terrace, it is not necessary to hold the fear that gutter water might pass through the tap. If you give perfume to someone it is not logical to suspect that your hand might emit the foul smell of the faeces. If you travel with a ticket in a train, it is not proper to suspect that the Ticket Checker might catch you. If the insight is deeply instilled in your heart and is not just a subject of rational understanding, if it is not superficial but deep rooted, then it is not necessary to sustain the fear as to whether you will be able to maintain the deep insight in times of adversity. When a dacoit suddenly comes in front of the police, instinctively the hands of the police reach the revolver tied around the waist.

Yours

## 68

**Dear Naman,**

I am bringing to your notice a mischief of the mind which we are unable to locate easily. It does not hold any doubt in inauspicious matters, whereas it does not hold trust in pious matters. When it has to tour Kashmir, it doesn't look out for an auspicious omen but before going on a pilgrimage, it likes to look out for an auspicious omen. Will I be able to re-collect the guidance provided to me regarding the attainment of monetary gains in my adversity?' This fear never tortures the mind. 'Will I be able to retain the spiritual guidance in pain and allurement? This fear keeps troubling it many a time. Don't sacrifice the pleasant and sound present in the scare of a bleak future. Have you heard the proverb 'Let's take the advantage of today. Who has seen tomorrow?' Have you heard the idiom 'we will face any kind of situation?' You might have also heard this 'Do it today which you have kept off for tomorrow, do it now which you have kept off for today.' Keeping all these idioms, proverbs etc. before your eyes, you proceed on with the aid of the deep insight you have attained today. As far as the future is concerned, even I don't know what tomorrow has in store for me? 'Where will I die? When will I die? In which situation will I die? Who will be near me at that time?' Though, I am unaware of all these, I am living my saintly life very happily. 'What is the secret of my happiness?' The in-depth belief that the action of today is the 'womb' for the creation of the 'future'. The prospects of the future are dependant on the deeds of today. If the decisive factor of my next birth is the state in which I die, then the state, in which I die is dependant on the way I live my life.

Naman, the destination might be thousands of miles away, but we have to tread one step at a time. The future might extend to infinite years, but we have to take care of the present moment only.

Yours

## 69

**Sir,**

Your valuable advice has removed my misconception. If a bowler is intent on taking the wicket of a batsman, he bowls each ball with attention. If a batsman wants to strike a century, he plays each ball with due caution. If a student wants to score highest marks, he solves each question patiently. If a truck driver wants to travel a distance of thousand kilometres, he drives the truck vigilantly each moment. Similarly, if I want a bright tomorrow, I must take care of today and each and every moment of today. Am I right?

Naman

# 70

**Dear Naman,**

Almighty God Shri Mahavir Swami had given the same advice to his first disciple ganadhar Shri Gautam Swami. 'समयं गोयम! मा पमायए' 'Gautam! Don't waste even a moment.' If this be the advice to a vigilant saint who never wasted even a second, then the advice to all of us, who spend most of the time in trivial and insignificant matters, would naturally be just the same.

Start implementing in the practical life, the deep insight obtained by you through the medium of correspondence. This world does not discuss about happiness and sorrow which play hide and seek game with the living beings. But the vital question is how many know the reason behind fortune and misfortune? Instill the deep belief in your heart that sorrow and happiness is a result of maleficent deed (Paap karma) and meritorious deed (Punya karma) respectively.

I am sure that as a result of this, you can't commit sins with delight. You can't stay without forsaking avoidable sins. You will grab the chance to perform religious deeds. You will be able to maintain uninterrupted piety and cheerfulness amidst the onslaughts of sorrow and happiness coming in your life as a result of past deeds committed by you.

In the court of your conscience, at anytime, at any place and under any circumstances, you can stand erect with absolute fearlessness. What else do you want in your life?

*Yours*

# 71

**Sir,**

It is true that the deep insight obtained by me is only at the mental scale now, but I have the firm faith that in the near future, I will put it into practice and experience the sweet taste of incessant happiness. I am well aware that I have to put in tremendous efforts to put it into practice. But then, the blessings of Lord Almighty and revered saints are with me. I am constantly receiving your valuable guidance in this regard. I am sure that with this invaluable support, I will certainly succeed in my efforts. Please shower your hearty blessings on me.

Naman

# 72

**Dear Naman,**

Not just you but even I am in need of blessings. A batsman scoring 100 runs in net practice might lose his wicket in the Test Match without scoring even a single run. A student obtaining 90% marks in the half yearly exams might fail in the Annual exams.

A driver driving safely up to 499 kilometres, might lose his life, if he dozes off in the last kilometres. he has to cover. Similarly, it's possible that the vast insight instilled deep in the mind for the entire life time might prove impotent in the critical period. Lest the deep insight might be forgotten, lest the deep insight might not become impotent. I, you and all of us must always crave for the blessings and good wishes of God and Gurudev so that our deep insight becomes impregnable in any situation. Have you heard this sentence? 'First you do what you can, and then God will do what you cannot.' The meaning is very clear.

Firstly put in your maximum efforts, when you are completely exhausted. Then God will come and finish the remaining work.

Naman, do not lack in efforts, do not compromise in developing worthiness and do not depend on good works and evildeeds. Then observe, how benevolently God showers his blessings on you!

Yours

## 73

**Sir,**

A red-hot coal might be lying near the river accidentally. Doesn't the river extinguish it? A man may trample a flower under his feet in a fit of rage, yet doesn't the flower leave its fragrance on his feet? A farmer might carelessly throw seeds in his farm, yet doesn't the farm offer him abundant crop in return? You have done just the same. I have filed our entire correspondance and numbered it. Yesterday in the night time, during leisure I was turning the pages of the file. My eyes fell on the first letter written to you. I read it quite patiently. Tears rolled down my eyes. In a fit of anger I had written the letter. Under the pretext of pain and agony, I raised childish arguments before you. 'Why has the burden of sorrow, misfortune fallen over me only?' 'Why is it that only I have become the target of injustice & insults?' 'Why am I only suppressed?' 'Why only I shed tears in lamentation?' Ferociously

O God! why me?

I charged one question after the other in my first letter, but ignoring my ferocity you patiently gave excellent solution to all my questions.

In each letter you had showered love and affection only. What a logical solution you had given to all my irrational questions. Showering on me the affection of a father sometimes and a mother at times, providing me the warmth of a friend at times, giving me the care of a sister, a brother at times, offering me the advice of a Guru at times, you gradually won my heart. I've become yours. O benevolent Sir ! Each drop of my blood, every thought of my mind, each and every spot of my soul is uttering incessantly the very same sentence, 'you are my greatest benefactor !'

If you grant a little space to this Naman in a corner of your heart, I will consider myself most fortunate.

Naman

## 74

**Dear Naman,**

Your previous letter shook me completely. Every word of your letter conveyed the message of gratitude and admiration. Your profound respect for me has naturally created a liking for you. Though, I have given a reasonable solution to the various questions raised by you in your first letter; today, on the event of a stand-still to our correspondence, I would like to unravel your perplexity with a different angle. Almighty God wants to include you in his family, so he has devised a method to bring you near him. To strengthen your tolerance power he sent an army of sorrow at your door step.

The Sovereign of religion (Dharma Satta) wants to free you from the bondage of deeds, so it has showered tons of misery on you through the medium of Sovereign of deeds (Karma Satta). To grant you incessant and infinite happiness the cosmic order is shoving off your sin (Pap Karma) by insulting you. To uplift you and bring you up to the level of his own status, God has sent the messenger 'sorrow' which will bring you nearer to him every minute.

Naman, Do you want to say anything in this regard?

Yours

## 75

**Sir,**

If this is the fact, then I would like to tell God 'O God! grant distress to me only.' I would like to tell 'Sovereign of religion', 'O Sovereign of religion! make only me the victim of difficulties and discomforts'. I would like to tell 'Sovereign of deeds', 'O Sovereign of deeds! you send all the troops of injustice and insults near me only.'

Firstly, I would like to reach God at the earliest and till I reach that honourable position, in each and every birth, I would like to submit my life to God only! After being freed from the intolerable torture of deeds and evil intuition, I would like to attain salvation at the earliest. Sir! what do you want to say in this regard?

Naman

# 76

**Dear Naman,**

I am elated to know that you are eager to obtain salvation at the earliest for this very purpose, I renounced the entire world. I earnestly pray God to grant (salvation) his status to you and me at the earliest.

Yours